POWERING SUCCESS SHAPING LEADERS

THE MENTOR ADVANTAGE

RICHA SINGH

Prologue

As I look back at my journey, and how I sailed through many failures and successes, I can't help but think of those people who were instrumental in shaping me and supporting me. I am not the sole architect of my successes. Along the way, I have encountered remarkable individuals—mentors, counselors, and managers—who took on the role of mentors and catalyzed a better version of me. Their presence, guidance, and unwavering support created a foundation upon which I built my confidence, overcame challenges, and achieved what I once thought impossible.

Whether it was personal lows or professional challenges, having someone who could provide that sanctuary—helping me see through the clouds with objectivity—made all the difference. They offered me the support to sail through turbulent waters or stay afloat when I felt like I might drown. These individuals listened without judgment, challenged me to introspect, and encouraged me to find clarity amidst chaos. Without them, I don't believe I would be the person I am today.

Looking back, I realize that mentors entered my life at pivotal moments—when I was struggling to find my footing, when my confidence faltered, and when I needed to make difficult choices. Their belief in me, even when I doubted myself, helped me bounce up and get going. They gave me the courage to face my fears, embrace my potential, and move forward with purpose.

This book is a tribute to those mentors, to the power of meaningful connections, and to the profound impact of a single conversation, a word of encouragement, or a listening ear. It is an invitation to reflect on the mentors in your own life, or perhaps, to seek one out. Because as I have learned, we all need someone who sees us for who we are and who we can become.

So, as you turn these pages, I hope you find inspiration in my journey and in the stories of mentorship that have shaped me. May they remind you of the importance of seeking support, embracing growth, and becoming a mentor to others. After all, our greatest achievements are rarely ours alone—they are the result of shared wisdom, guidance, and the courage to keep moving forward.

A Note of Thanks

Life has been a journey full of challenges and triumphs, moments of doubt and sparks of inspiration. Over the years, I encountered both personal and professional hurdles that tested my strength and resolve. I survived, and I flourished, not only due to my resolve but also due to support and guidance of mentors I found along the way.

There were times, when I didn't even realize that I needed a hand to pull me out and help me fly, I was lucky and the universe seemed to know. It sent mentors when I needed guidance the most and counselors when my mind was clouded with turmoil. These serendipitous connections became lifelines, helping me navigate my path, and they taught me that support often comes not when we seek it, but when we need it most.

This book is dedicated to those remarkable individuals who believed in me, guided me, and stood by me, helping me emerge stronger and happier. To them, I owe the clarity to see my potential and the courage to embrace it. They are the reason I stand here today, sharing my journey with you.

First and foremost, I am who I am today because of my family. My mother, whose strength has always been my anchor. My sister and my dad, who have been my steadfast supporters. My two boys, Arun and Varun, who fill my world with love, laughter, and purpose every single day. And, of course, my two dogs, Buddy and Coco, who are bundles of energy filling our hearts and home with their unconditional love.

I am deeply grateful to my friends who became pillars of strength during my personal chaos, offering wisdom and guidance that served a ray of hope. Their unwavering loyalty and support in countless battles, standing firmly by me and my family, will forever be cherished. To those who, without the formal title of mentor, shared their kindness and wisdom, your impact on my journey has been invaluable, and I carry profound gratitude in my heart.

Then there are those who took on the mantle of mentors and counselors, shaping my professional journey and helping me see beyond the immediate challenges. It is impossible to capture the depth of my gratitude in words, but I hope this book serves as a testament to the invaluable role they played in my life.

To everyone who has been a part of my story, thank you. This book is as much yours as it is mine, a celebration of the power of connection, the beauty of shared wisdom, and the resilience that mentorship inspires.

A special thanks to my mentors.

Nodjame Fouad, CEO Irish Distillers

For helping me address my fears, open up and introspect and find ways to be a better leader, a mother and be at peace with myself for choices I had made.

Dr Niru Kumar, Padma Shri, 2021. CEO Ask Insights

For being an inspiration and a sounding board, and helping me through some of my toughest personal challenges. For helping me objectively assess what my life was offering, appreciate that, and embrace happiness over regret and misery.

Helene De Tissot, Group CFO, Pernod Ricard

For encouraging candid discussions and vulnerability, in trying times at work and some speedy tips to navigate a very new world for me, during our short interactions over the last few years.

Jean Touboul, CEO Pernod Ricard India

For giving me a canvas to paint, being a sounding board, trusting me and helping me appreciate very diverse views- and sometimes – a man's side of things.

Gurprriet Singh, Managing Director, Russell Reynolds, India

For helping me see my potential and put away my fears, some of which were unfounded, and for encouraging me to focus on where I want to be and what can get me there, I am deeply grateful. Introduced to me by Nitu Bhushan, who brought him onboard for leadership counseling, he initially faced my resistance to opening up. Yet, with patience and insight, he broke through those walls, becoming a guiding force who reminded me to trust the process, believe in myself, and embrace the path to growth with clarity and purpose.

And lastly my friend and colleague,

Nitu Bhushan CHRO, Pernod Ricard India

For standing by me in testing times, and opening the doors to mentorship for me, introducing me to mentors that once again gave me wings to fly, pulling me out of my lows.

How to Read This Book

This book is designed as a guide for anyone curious about possibilities with mentoring. If you've ever found yourself wondering whether mentoring really works or how to make the most of a mentor, this book provides insights and inspiration. Perhaps you've asked yourself, what could I possibly gain from having a mentor, or what should I even do with one? These are natural questions, and they're precisely what this book aims to address.

The book starts with a mini first section that lays out the basics of mentoring and being mentored. This is followed by a section with my stories and small personal illustrations, demonstrating how conversations with mentors can catalyze self-improvement in ways you might not have achieved on your own. Mentors often act as mirrors and guides, helping us to see possibilities, navigate challenges, and refine our goals. This book offers a glimpse into real-life moments where mentoring has sparked growth, clarity, and change. Last section is a call to action, to embrace mentoring as a way to be on a lifelong process of self-reflection and improvement.

The narrative is light and approachable, making it an easy and engaging read. It's an invitation to reflect on whether you want to create a support system around yourself and how such a group can profoundly impact your personal and professional journey.

Additionally, this book is useful for both those seeking to be mentors and those considering mentoring as a path to personal growth. For aspiring mentors, it provides insights into the subtle yet impactful role they can play in guiding others. The book illustrates how mentors, through gentle prodding and thoughtful conversations, can help mentees unravel their doubts, uncover hidden potentials, and find solutions they might not have reached alone.

For mentees, it emphasizes the importance of opening—sharing their challenges, dreams, and uncertainties to fully harness the benefits of the mentoring relationship. By doing so, mentees can unlock the power of self-reflection and growth, facilitated by the safe and encouraging space a mentor provides.

As you read, allow yourself to think about your own life and the potential role mentors or support groups could play in it. This book isn't just about mentoring; it's about exploring how meaningful connections can help us become the best versions of ourselves.

So settle in, enjoy the stories, and let them inspire you to take the next step in building your own circle of growth and support.

Index

A mentor's role is to guide and empower mentees to find their unique path through listening, empathy, and constructive guidance.

Begin mentoring by choosing the right mentor, building rapport, sharing challenges, and gradually aligning goals for transformative growth.

Overcoming introversion and learning the importance of visibility and collaboration in professional growth.

Ending Note

Positivity and acceptance drive resilience and clarity, empowering individuals to achieve success and fulfilment while inspiring change.

Section 1

Getting started

Being a Mentor:

Mentoring is an art developed through experience, where a mentor is solely focused on helping their mentee overcome self-limiting fears and behaviors to reach their potential.

Mentorship is not just about helping you with professional growth; it's about creating a safe space where apprehensions are shared, vulnerabilities are embraced, and solutions are discovered.

It doesn't require special qualifications or certifications. What it does require is experience, the ability to listen deeply, and, most importantly, the ability to appreciate the mentee's uniqueness. Being a good mentor means understanding that there is no one-size-fits-all solution to life's challenges. Instead, mentoring is about guiding the mentee to find their own path, helping them arrive at the right solutions without prescribing answers.

One needs to choose a mentor carefully. Along with experience, your mentor should have time to see you through your challenges in a way that works for you.

Earlier in life, I met a mentor, I thought I could trust immediately. She had the charisma, the title, and an impressive track record. During our initial conversations, I eagerly shared my challenges and frustrations. I had quit my job, to look after my twin toddlers. I wasn't sure if I will ever be able to get back to my career. Personally, life wasn't going too well, I was caught up in a negative spiral in my marriage. She heard me patiently, and then narrated her own challenges, and how she had overcome them, which was inspiring.

However, she then became prescriptive. She simply told me what to do. It sounded too drastic to me; and I felt she doesn't really understand my circumstances. I wasn't ready to take those steps. I heard her out and left. I never met her after this incident.

Today I know, her advice was right, and I would have been better off, had I followed it. It might have landed better with me, had she made me think through on how I could end the negative spiral I was in, and things I would need to take care of, if I was to do so. Asking me, if that's what I wanted, and if I could do it, and gradually working with me through the solution, would have been a better approach.

I also had some amazing mentors, who saw me through my hurdles. They took the time to understand my unique challenges, not just professionally but personally. They would ask thought-provoking questions: "What's holding you back?" or "How do you envision success for yourself?" These conversations felt like a partnership rather than a lecture.

One critical factor in a successful mentoring relationship is alignment. A good mentor not only understands your goals but also has enough experience in your field to offer relevant insights. I once worked with a mentor who, despite their best intentions, had very little understanding of the nature of my work. While he was kind and empathetic, his guidance often felt out of sync with the challenges I faced. It made me realize how crucial it is to have a mentor who can understand the nuances of your specific professional context.

Today I have a mentor who has walked a similar path in my industry. Her advice is grounded in practical experience, making it both actionable and deeply impactful. She is able to anticipate the challenges I might face and provide strategies to work around. them effectively.

The key is balance: a mentor should have the expertise to guide you but also the humility to recognize that your journey is unique. They should inspire you to think critically, explore possibilities, and make decisions that align with your authentic self.

I am sharing below a small check list of things one should avoid as mentor and a reference list of questions mentors usually use to help one reflect and find answers.

Things a Mentor Should Never Do:

1. **Impose Their Solutions:** Mentoring is not about handing out pre-packaged solutions or insisting the mentee follow a specific path. Every mentee is unique, and what worked for the mentor may not work for them.

2. **Dominate the Conversation:** A mentor who talks too much, risks overshadowing the mentee's voice. Mentoring should empower the mentee to articulate their thoughts and find their own answers.

3. **Judge or Criticize:** Creating a judgment-free space is essential. Criticism, even if well-intentioned, can shut down open communication and make the mentee hesitant to share.

4. **Dismiss Emotions:** Mentors should acknowledge and validate the mentee's feelings, even if they don't fully understand them. Dismissing emotions can make the mentee feel unheard or unsupported.

5. **Push Their Agenda:** Mentoring is about the mentee's goals and challenges, not about the mentor's aspirations for them. A good mentor resists the temptation to steer the mentee toward outcomes that align with their own values or beliefs.

6. **Overstep Boundaries:** Respecting the mentee's privacy and autonomy is critical. A mentor should never pry into areas the mentee isn't ready to discuss or try to control their decisions.

Questions to Help Mentees Think and Share:

Good mentors ask thoughtful, open-ended questions to spark deeper reflection and understanding. Here are some examples:

- **Clarifying Goals:**

  - What do you want to achieve in the next year? Five years?

  - What does success look like for you in this situation?

- **Exploring Challenges:**

  - What's the biggest obstacle you're facing right now?

  - How have you tried to address this challenge so far?

  - What's holding you back from taking the next step?

- **Uncovering Motivations:**

  - Why is this goal important to you?

  - What excites you most about this opportunity?

  - What's at stake if you don't address this?

- **Encouraging Reflection:**

  - How do you feel about the choices you've made so far?

  - What's one thing you wish you had done differently?

  - What did you learn from that experience?

- **Fostering Creativity:**

  - What are some alternative approaches you could consider?

  - If you weren't afraid of failing, what would you try?

  - Who else might you involve to gain fresh perspectives?

- **Focusing on Action:**

  - What's one small step you can take today to move forward?

  - Who can support you in reaching this goal?

  - How will you measure progress and know when you've succeeded?

Building Trust and Connection:

A good mentoring relationship thrives on trust and mutual respect. Mentors should:

- **Listen Actively:** Show genuine interest in what the mentee is saying. Use verbal and non-verbal cues to convey attentiveness.

- **Be Vulnerable:** Share their own challenges and failures when appropriate. Vulnerability fosters connection and helps mentees feel less alone in their struggles, and also open up.

- **Encourage Autonomy:** Support the mentee in making their own decisions, even if they might disagree with the mentor's perspective.

- **Follow Through:** If a mentor commits to helping in a specific way—like introducing the mentee to a contact or providing resources—it's crucial to deliver on that promise.

Good mentoring has the power to transform lives. By asking the right questions, sharing insights thoughtfully, and empowering mentees to take ownership of their journeys, mentors can inspire confidence and unlock potential. At its heart, mentoring is a partnership—a shared journey of discovery and growth that benefits both mentor and mentee.

It's important for mentors to help mentee's open up to be able to address their issues and guide them on the right path.

I once mentored a young manager. He seemed depressed, didn't talk much, and his manager had been complaining of "attitude issues". While I couldn't gauge what was bogging him down, I knew he was not in a good place. I shared with me about some rough patches in my life, and a time when I was going through a rough patch with my boss. I then asked him to share his story, and how he was feeling at work.

Empathizing with me, he finally spoke. He said, he liked his manager, but at the same time resented her. She was young, nearly his age. He had worked longer, yet he was not getting promoted, and now that she was here- it would be several years before he could get promoted.

That resentment was pushing him down, making things worse, and potentially taking the promotion further away from him. The fix was simple. I encouraged him to have an open conversation with his manager and agree on a list of projects which he would excel in to succeed to the next level, along with timelines that worked with both. Once that was done, I suggested he also take feedback and inputs with his other stakeholders including his next level manager.

Things worked out. He found an ally in his manager, and was back, chalking out his growth story.

Fixes and solutions are often simple. Mentors help do away with clouds of doubt and confusion to help mentees succeed in their purpose.

How to Get Started on a Mentoring Journey:

Embarking on a mentoring journey can be one of the most enriching decisions you make for your personal and professional growth. It can be little confusing at first, if we are not very clear of our purpose, or have reflected on what holds us back, or things that bog us down. The thought of opening to someone we do not know too well, may also be a little discomforting to some.

To set yourself up for success, it's essential to approach the process with intention and openness. Here are some steps to help you get started:

1. **Choose the Right Mentor:** Select someone who isn't directly involved in your daily work but understands your professional and personal context. This ensures they can provide objective insights without being entangled in your immediate workplace dynamics. Look for someone whose experience, values, and approach resonate with your goals.

2. **Use the Initial Sessions to Build Rapport:** The first few mentoring sessions are crucial for establishing a

strong foundation. Take the time to get to know each other as individuals. Share your background, values, and interests. Opening up about your dreams and aspirations can help your mentor understand what drives you and where you hope to go.

3. **Start Small: Share Your Challenges:** Once you've built rapport, you can start introducing the challenges or concerns you face. If you're unclear about areas to work on, or things to discuss, reflect on feedback you've received or situations that leave you feeling stuck or worried. Discussing these can provide a starting point for deeper exploration and guidance.

4. **Gradually Focus on Your Goals:** As the relationship develops, shift the focus toward where you want to be and what might hold you back from achieving your goals. Collaborate with your mentor to identify actionable steps to overcome these barriers.

5. **Consider Personality or Leadership Assessments for Clarity:** If you're uncertain about your strengths, limitations, or areas for improvement, tools like 360-degree assessments or psychometric tests can offer valuable insights. These aren't mandatory but can provide a helpful baseline for self-awareness and growth.

6. **The Secret to Successful Mentoring:** The key to a successful mentoring relationship lies in your willingness to open up. Share your limitations

honestly and articulate where you aspire to go. Transparency fosters trust and allows your mentor to offer targeted guidance and support.

Remember, mentoring is a partnership. Approach it with curiosity, commitment, and a readiness to learn, and you'll discover how profoundly it can shape your journey toward personal and professional fulfilment.

Section 2

My Stories, Reflections and The Mentor Advantage

Early Years:

I wasn't a smooth sailor. Despite graduating from IIM, while most of my batchmates seemed to breeze through their early careers, I found myself struggling to find my footing. With little prior work experience and my natural introversion, I felt lost in the corporate world. I was technically sound, often producing the best reports and solutions, yet compared to my peers, I wasn't making much of an impact.

There were some critical yet understated aspects of corporate life that weren't obvious to me. I didn't understand the importance of creating buy-in for my ideas, the power of networking, or even the need to showcase my work. I assumed good work would speak for itself, but I remained invisible.

I kept my head down, working in isolation, avoiding corridor and coffee conversations, and missing out on the benefits of forming connections. No matter how strong my output, recognition rarely came my way. Over time, this eroded my confidence, leaving me feeling adrift.

Early in my career, I struggled under the weight of managers who couldn't see past my introversion. To them, I was an enigma—an employee who delivered strong results but didn't fit their mold of what a team member should be. Their frustration was evident, and instead of helping me grow, they distanced themselves. This, in turn, caused me to withdraw even further, trapping me in a cycle of self-doubt and isolation.

But then, as if fortune had finally smiled on me, I met the managers who became my "coaches." These extraordinary individuals didn't see my introversion as a limitation but as an untapped strength. They took the time to understand me, patiently uncovering my potential where others had seen only barriers. They didn't dismiss me as "too quiet" or "not a fit." Instead, they taught me how to embrace my unique abilities, amplifying my strengths and showing me how to grow with confidence and purpose. Their belief in me transformed the trajectory of my career and reshaped my belief in myself.

One instance remains etched in my memory. After a senior management meeting where I fumbled due to nerves, my manager took me out for a drink. He asked, "What happened in there?" I admitted that the meeting hadn't gone well and fell silent, unsure of what more to say.

He didn't reprimand me. Instead, he shared a piece of advice that changed everything.

"Richa, if you want a seat at that table, they need to see you as their equal." He then pointed out a senior colleague and encouraged me to observe how they conducted themselves.

That conversation was a turning point. For the first time, I felt like someone truly believed in me. My manager wasn't just giving feedback; he was empowering me to step up and claim my space. He became my guardian angel, guiding me through meetings, presentations, and professional challenges with unwavering support.

I learned that it wasn't enough to have the right answers; I needed to involve others, build consensus, and create advocates for my ideas. These lessons, though simple, were profound.

Under the guidance of these nurturing managers, I began to blossom. They helped me see that my introversion wasn't a weakness—it was simply a different way of engaging with the world. By teaching me how to package my strengths and navigate the unspoken rules of corporate life, they reignited my confidence.

I started to approach meetings and presentations as opportunities to shine rather than events to dread. I embraced collaboration and networking, recognizing that the most significant achievements often come from collective effort and support of one's colleagues and seniors.

Today, I carry these lessons into my own leadership. I strive to be the kind of manager who nurtures and supports younger team members, showing them the way when they feel lost. Like my mentors, I aim to see the potential in others and help them unlock it.

Everyone needs a mentor to survive and succeed. The needs may vary depending on where we are in our growth journeys, but the impact of a supportive guide is universal.

Key Takeaways:

1. **Recognize the Power of Mentorship:** Mentors can transform your career by helping you see your potential, offering guidance, and opening doors to opportunities.

2. **Networking Matters:** Building connections is as important as producing results. Collaborate, involve

others in your ideas, and create advocates for your work.

3. **Speak Up and Show Up:** No matter how strong your output, visibility and confidence are essential to making an impact.

4. **Value Nurturing Leadership:** A good manager doesn't just evaluate performance—they nurture talent, guide growth, and inspire confidence.

5. **Pay It Forward:** Take the lessons you've learned from your mentors and apply them to those who look up to you. Being a mentor is a way of honoring those who guided you.

Ambition:

Breaking Barriers: Finding Courage

I have always been ambitious, eager to embrace new roles and challenge myself with bigger tasks. I thrive on finding the best solutions to help businesses succeed. Leading with purpose, I take pride in my ability to infuse passion in teams, fostering a winning culture that drives results. However, despite my accomplishments, I found myself increasingly uncertain about my future.

While I enjoyed my work and performed well, a deeper part of me was excited by something else—an unspoken dream that I feared to voice. I knew, deep down, that if given the opportunity, I could excel. Yet, I hesitated to speak up. Would sharing my aspirations impact my career negatively? Would it undermine the work I was already doing? These questions held me back.

At this stage of my career, with about a third of my employable years left, I found myself in a paradox. On one hand, I had amassed a wealth of experience and could contribute at a higher level. On the other, I viewed time as slipping away—a glass half full that left me feeling insecure. I didn't want my climb to plateau; I wanted to keep rising.

Around this time, I got picked up for Global Mentorship Program. Initially, I wasn't sure on how I would gain from it. It started with a small warm up chat and introductions. It might have been obvious, that I was holding myself back. It was my mentor who helped ease me into our conversations and gave me the courage to open. For the first time, I shared what truly drove me. Initially, my thoughts were jumbled, and I worried I sounded confused. Self-doubt crept in, making me question whether I even had the right to dream of something different.

But my mentor didn't let me stay in that space. She asked the right questions, challenging me to reflect deeply on what I truly wanted. What would make me happy each day? Slowly, I found the clarity to articulate my aspirations. Armed with this newfound understanding, I mustered the courage to share my goals with my manager.

The conversation with my manager didn't lead to any overnight changes or gains. He listened but made no immediate promises. Yet, just expressing myself was a relief. It felt as though a weight had been lifted from my shoulders. For the first time, I was at peace with where I was and what I was doing.

I realized that if I continued to excel in my current role while staying open to learning and growth, opportunities would eventually align with my goals. More importantly, the people who mattered now knew what I wanted. They would see my commitment and readiness when the right moment arrived.

Mentoring taught me the power of vulnerability and self-awareness. It gave me the confidence to confront my fears and speak my truth. My journey with my mentor not only helped me align my career with my deeper aspirations but also inspired me to encourage others to embrace mentoring. Sometimes, all it takes is one conversation—one person who believes in you—to transform your perspective and propel you toward your dreams.

Key Takeaways:

1. **Acknowledging Inner Desires is the First Step:** Recognizing and confronting your deeper aspirations—even if they feel unclear or intimidating—is vital for personal and professional growth.

2. **Fear of Judgment Can Hinder Growth:** Unspoken fears about how sharing aspirations might be perceived can block progress. A safe and supportive environment, like mentoring, helps break this cycle.

3. **Mentoring Sparks Clarity:** A mentor's guidance and probing questions can help untangle thoughts and bring clarity to aspirations and goals.

4. **Vulnerability Builds Strength:** Opening up about uncertainties or dreams is not a sign of weakness but a step toward aligning your career with your true passions.

5. **Communicating Goals is Empowering:** Sharing aspirations with key stakeholders, such as managers, creates awareness and lays the groundwork for future opportunities, even if immediate changes don't occur.

6. **Self-Reflection Fuels Growth:** Taking time to reflect on your journey through mentorship enables self-awareness and builds confidence to take actionable steps toward personal and professional fulfilment.

7. **The Ripple Effect of Mentoring:** Mentoring doesn't just transform individuals; it also inspires them to become advocates for mentoring, creating a culture of support and growth.

Building High-Performing Teams, Balancing Inclusivity and Accountability:

I take immense pride in building and leading winning teams, rooted in openness and collaboration. For me, a winning team embodies a relentless drive to improve and deliver—quarter after quarter, always aiming higher. Even while leading a finance function, which doesn't directly produce or ship products, there is immense potential to make an impact. Whether it's driving cost improvements, enhancing audit quality, or developing robust analytics to influence stronger decisions on pricing or targets, there is always room to push the boundaries of excellence.

My teams have often been energized and eager to win, striving for recognition and meaningful contributions. However, as I began to lead larger teams, I encountered new challenges. Not everyone thrives in a high-pressure, success-driven environment. Some team members burn out, while others—the derailers—may resist or even hinder progress.

When I encountered derailers, I often found myself less tolerant, usually trying to minimize my interaction with them. This worried me. As a compassionate leader, I knew this approach could further affect their morale and might even seem unfair. Yet, derailers often challenged my value system, which triggered my reactions.

I wanted to be a more inclusive leader—someone who could balance the drive for results with empathy, ensuring no one felt alienated. At the same time, I needed to maintain a strong focus on performance without compromising the team's overall success.

If a manager fails to stay neutral and treats team members with varying degrees of tolerance or patience, several negative outcomes can arise:

1. **Perceived Favoritism:** Inconsistent behavior can lead to perceptions of favoritism. When team members feel that others are receiving more leniency or support, it can breed resentment and undermine trust. This creates divisions within the team and hinders collaboration.

2. **Eroding Morale:** If certain individuals feel singled out or unfairly treated, their morale and motivation are likely to decline. Over time, this can result in disengagement and lower productivity, affecting the team's overall performance.

3. **Impact on Culture:** A lack of objectivity can erode the culture of fairness and openness that high-performing teams need to thrive. Team members may become hesitant to voice concerns, offer feedback, or take risks, fearing inconsistent reactions.

4. **Reduced Credibility:** Managers who display bias or inconsistency risk losing credibility. Once team members perceive a lack of fairness, it becomes challenging for the manager to effectively lead, inspire, or make impactful decisions.

5. To mitigate these risks, it is crucial for managers to ensure their behavior, decisions, and actions equally reflect objectivity. This means:

- **Consistent Standards:** Setting clear performance expectations and applying them uniformly to all team members helps eliminate ambiguity and ensures fairness.

- **Empathetic Listening:** Taking the time to understand individual challenges while maintaining the same level of patience with everyone fosters trust and inclusivity.

- **Transparent Decision-Making:** Clearly communicating the rationale behind decisions minimizes misunderstandings and reinforces confidence in leadership.

- **Regular Self-Reflection:** Managers must regularly assess whether their actions align with their values and the principles of fairness they aim to uphold.

When I brought this challenge to my mentor, I found myself unraveling emotions I hadn't fully acknowledged before. I spoke about how derailers—those who resisted or hindered progress—had an outsized impact on me. Their behavior triggered something deeper, leading me to respond differently than I would with others.

I told her, "Despite my commitment to objectivity in decision-making and impartiality in work, I noticed a pattern: I would instinctively minimize my interactions with them. It wasn't deliberate, but it was there, and it bothered me. As a leader, I had always prided myself on fairness and empathy, yet this behavior felt out of alignment with the values I held so dear.

What troubled me most was the fear of how it might be perceived. Could my actions appear biased or unfair? Was I unintentionally creating a gap between my intent and my actions? Deep down, I knew I wasn't biased—my decisions were always grounded in fairness—but perception is powerful, and I didn't want even a shadow of doubt to linger."

Talking it through with my mentor helped me confront this blind spot. It wasn't about questioning my principles—they were intact—but about ensuring my actions consistently reflected the fairness and inclusivity I wanted to embody as a leader.

My mentor helped me explore some key concerns:

- Was I right in addressing derailers or team members who couldn't meet expectations?

- Was my frustration with low performers affecting my interactions with them?

- Was my approach too rigid compared to other managers who seemed more flexible with underperformance?

Through my discussions with my mentor, I began to understand why derailers had such a profound impact on me. It stemmed from a clash of value systems. I held certain principles—accountability, ownership, and mutual respect—in the highest regard, and when those values were challenged, it triggered an emotional response that influenced my behavior. My mentor helped me see that as a leader, it's essential to stay objective about performance, recognizing that people have different drivers, reactions, and ways of expressing themselves.

Instead of judging derailers for their actions or taking their behavior personally, I needed to rewire my approach. This meant staying laser-focused on what I needed from them in terms of performance, while still nurturing close, supportive bonds with my team. It required a shift in mindset—one that emphasized separating actions from individuals and addressing issues with clarity and purpose. I also came to realize that people respond differently to challenges, success, or failure, and my role as a leader wasn't to judge these reactions but to align everyone around a common purpose. By staying objective and addressing the issues that impacted team performance, I could lead with both empathy and accountability, ensuring no one felt alienated while still maintaining high standards.

Reflecting and working through these challenges helped me grow as a leader—balancing inclusivity with accountability to build a resilient, high-performing team.

Key Takeaways:

1. **Winning Teams Require Constant Growth:** Even in roles that are not directly customer-facing, such as finance, there is always room to innovate, refine, and contribute to broader organizational success. Leaders should embrace this mindset and encourage their teams to do the same.

2. **Not Everyone Thrives Under Pressure:** While high-performing teams often attract individuals eager for

recognition and achievement, some team members may struggle or resist. Recognizing and addressing this dynamic is crucial for maintaining team morale and productivity.

3. **The Importance of Self-Reflection for Leaders:** Mentoring sessions or designated "think time" provide leaders with the opportunity to reflect on their leadership styles, identify areas for improvement, and develop strategies to address challenges.

4. **Empathy Does Not Mean Lowering Standards:** Inclusive leadership is about balancing empathy with accountability. Leaders can support team members by addressing performance issues with clarity, fairness, and respect, without compromising on expectations or team goals.

5. **Performance Discussions Must Be Objective:** Clear and transparent communication about expectations and consequences is essential. Leaders should focus on addressing performance issues constructively, ensuring personal relationships do not cloud judgment.

6. **Difficult Decisions Are Part of Leadership:** At times, leaders may need to transition underperforming team members to roles that better suit their capabilities— or, in some cases, make the tough call for them to exit the organization. Doing so with fairness and respect strengthens the team in the long run.

7. **Growth Happens Through Challenges:** By addressing their own frustrations and learning to lead with both firmness and empathy, leaders grow personally and professionally, ultimately creating stronger, more resilient teams.

Influencing:

The Subtle Art of Influence

Influencing others is an essential leadership skill, but one that often comes with challenges and frustrations. I've always considered myself an open, straightforward person—someone who values facts, experience, and clear communication. I took pride in coming prepared to every discussion, armed with data and insights to drive decisions that I believed would benefit the organization. Yet, despite my efforts, I frequently found myself at a loss when my ideas were met with inexplicable resistance.

The most frustrating part was that I *knew* these ideas could work. I had analyzed the problems, weighed the risks, and developed well-thought-out solutions. But instead of sparking meaningful dialogue, my approach often felt like hitting a brick wall. Decisions stalled, and my passion for pushing the right course of action was misunderstood as being overly forceful or rigid.

This frustration was something I brought up with my mentor during one of our sessions. I laid out my challenges in detail:

- The roadblocks I faced despite being well-prepared.

- My efforts to build relationships and networks to make stakeholders more open to my ideas.

- The overwhelming sense of defeat when my contributions weren't adopted, even when they seemed to be in the best interest of the business.

It was clear to my mentor that my passion to drive business and solutions was spilling over into how I communicated. After hearing me out, she paused and said something I wasn't expecting:

"Maybe you're being too strong in how you present your ideas. Could it be that your passion is unintentionally making others feel backed into a corner? Leaders, especially veterans, might hear your approach as: 'This is what you *must* do,' rather than, 'Here's something to consider.' That could trigger a defensive reaction—they might feel like accepting your idea means admitting they couldn't solve the problem themselves. Could you try landing your ideas differently?"

Her advice was simple but profound. She suggested I shift my approach from passionately pitching a solution to presenting it as one of several options. "Take your passion out of it for a moment," she said, "and allow the other person to feel like it's their idea. It might take away the thrill of saying, 'This was *my* solution,' but it ensures the right thing is done for the business."

This hit me like a bolt of lightning. I realized my eagerness to solve problems had inadvertently made others feel cornered. My directness, which I had always considered a strength, might have come across as inflexibility or even arrogance. Leaders, especially those with years of experience, didn't want to feel they were being told what to do.

I reflected on this and saw the pattern clearly. My passion for driving results, while well-intentioned, had sometimes closed doors instead of opening them. The missed opportunities weren't because my ideas were flawed; they were because of how I was presenting them.

So, I decided to try a different approach. The next time I needed to influence a decision, I presented my idea as one of several possible solutions. I took a step back and asked questions like, "What do you think about this option?" or "Could this be a way forward?" This shift wasn't about diminishing my contributions but about giving others the space to feel ownership over the solution.

Conversations became more collaborative, decisions moved forward more smoothly, and I felt less frustrated. By taking the spotlight off myself and focusing on the bigger picture, I found that my ideas gained traction more easily.

This simple tweak in my approach—a shift from pushing to guiding—became a game-changer. It taught me that influence isn't about being the loudest voice in the room or proving that you're right. It's about creating an environment where the best ideas, regardless of their origin, can take root and flourish.

Through this experience, I learned a valuable lesson: Sometimes, letting go of the need for credit is the most effective way to lead. When you stop pushing and start enabling, the real magic happens—not just for the business, but for everyone involved.

Stepping back isn't always easy, but it's this very act of empowering others that transforms a manager into a true leader.

Key Takeaways: The Subtle Art of Influence:

1. **Passion vs. Push:** While passion for your ideas is important, pushing too strongly can unintentionally create resistance. Others might perceive your enthusiasm as inflexibility or as undermining their own expertise.

2. **Adopt a Collaborative Approach:** Frame your ideas as options rather than directives. Encourage discussion by asking open-ended questions like, "What do you think of this approach?" This invites collaboration and reduces defensiveness.

3. **Step Back to Move Forward:** Let go of the need to take credit for the idea. Focus on enabling others to take ownership, which often leads to quicker buy-in and better outcomes.

4. **Empathy in Communication:** Recognize that stakeholders may have their own perspectives and challenges. Tailor your messaging to align with their priorities and frame your suggestions in a way that resonates with their goals.

5. **Relationships Matter:** Building trust and understanding with stakeholders is crucial. Strong relationships make it easier for others to be receptive to your ideas.

6. **The Power of Simplicity:** Sometimes, the solution to complex challenges is a simple shift in mindset or approach. Influencing effectively is less about

proving you're right and more about guiding others toward the best decision.

7. **Leaders Enable, Not Dominate:** True influence comes from empowering others, not from being the loudest or most persistent voice in the room. Leadership is about creating a space where the best ideas can emerge and thrive.

Bias for Speed:

Speed has always been my ally. From the earliest days of school, it set me apart. I was the first to walk out of examination halls. One of my favorite stories to recount—and one I still take pride in—is completing my Class 10th math board exam in just 45 minutes, for a paper designed to last 90; and excelling in it.

My teachers often paused mid-sentence as I rattled off answers, well ahead of my peers. Speed was my superpower, a source of confidence and accomplishment.

In my early career, this strength served me well. As an individual contributor, my knack for quick thinking, decision-making, and execution allowed me to take on more work and exceed expectations. My managers were delighted with my efficiency and reliability. Even as a young manager, speed helped me shoulder additional responsibilities and deliver results. But as I progressed in my career, the very trait that had propelled me forward began to show its limitations.

As I moved into more senior roles, my bias for speed became a double-edged sword. I found myself completing tasks and clearing my plate while my team was still grappling with theirs. Often, I had idle moments between meetings, where I felt restless and unproductive. This led me to take on more work rather than delegating, a decision I justified as "speeding things up."

This preference for speed also influenced my behavior in meetings. Sitting in discussions, I would quickly assess the challenge at hand, and my mind would instinctively leap to solutions or what needed to happen next. While the rest of the team was still mulling over the issue, I often switched off and began attending to my emails or other tasks. Despite being a coach and mentor to many, I was oblivious to the impact this behavior had on those around me. Some team members felt offended, interpreting my disengagement as a sign that I didn't value their input. Others assumed I had nothing meaningful to contribute. Worst of all, it sometimes prevented me from steering conversations or guiding the team effectively.

Though I still haven't fully reined in my natural processing speed, I'm beginning to be mindful of the need to stay engaged in longer meetings. Even when I believe I've grasped everything, I remind myself that my colleagues might need time to process at their own pace—and that my presence and attention can influence the tone and outcomes of our discussions. I am very much a work in progress, but the conscious effort is helping.

Over time, I began to realize that my approach to speed created friction in other ways, too. I expected rapid-fire updates in meetings and wanted discussions to be swift and succinct, allowing me to pack in more tasks, meetings, and decisions. While my team worked hard to match my pace, I could sense their discomfort. They rarely voiced concerns, as we were achieving results and winning together, but the strain was palpable. The constant pressure to keep up with my tempo started to wear on both them and me.

I began to see that, I was burning out, caught in a cycle of doing and delegating halfway, only to see things slow down again. My love for speed, once my greatest strength, was now a source of dissatisfaction and diminishing returns.

Though I don't recall explicitly discussing my struggles with my mentor, our conversations over months provided clarity. Observing her was an education in itself. She had an incredible ability to be present, fully and completely, in every interaction. When we spoke, her focus was unwavering. There was no rush, no sense of urgency to move on to the next thing. That sense of calm and complete attention gave me comfort and trust.

Her demeanor made me reflect on my own approach. I started to see how my impatience and drive for speed might be affecting my team. It became clear that I needed to adjust, not just for their sake but for the overall effectiveness of our work.

I consciously began to slow down. I resisted the urge to take back work to expedite it. Instead, I encouraged my team to handle tasks at their pace, even if it felt slower to me. In meetings, I made a deliberate effort to give people time to express their thoughts fully, without rushing them to get to the point. It wasn't easy. I had to remind myself repeatedly that slowing down these moments was essential for better outcomes.

Timelines remained important, but I let go of the need to accelerate them unnecessarily. This shift wasn't about abandoning my love for speed; it was about finding balance. I realized that by slowing down strategically, I could create space for my team to breathe, think, and perform at their best.

This perceived slowdown brought unexpected benefits. Conversations with my team became more meaningful and insightful. They felt comfortable sharing their thoughts and concerns, knowing they had my full attention. This openness fostered better collaboration and led to more innovative solutions. By giving them the time and space to contribute fully, I not only improved our working relationships but also unlocked their potential in ways I hadn't anticipated.

My team still recognizes my penchant for speed, but they also know they have the freedom to pace their work according to their priorities and capacities. The balance we've struck has made us more effective as a group, delivering better results without the constant pressure of racing against the clock.

Slowing down doesn't mean sacrificing efficiency or productivity. On the contrary, it can lead to deeper understanding, stronger connections, and more sustainable success. My journey from speed-driven urgency to intentional pacing has taught me that sometimes, the fastest way to get somewhere is to go slow. By making space for thoughtfulness and collaboration, I've discovered a new kind of speed—one that's measured not in minutes saved, but in the quality and impact of the work we do together.

Key Takeaways:

1. **Strength of Speed:** Speed can be a powerful trait that sets individuals apart, enabling them to excel in tasks, meet goals quickly, and gain early recognition.

2. **The Double-Edged Sword:** While speed can drive efficiency, over-reliance on it may lead to challenges in collaborative and leadership contexts, such as disengagement or misalignment with team dynamics.

3. **Awareness of Impact:** Behaviors driven by a bias for speed, such as disengaging in discussions or multitasking during meetings, can unintentionally create misunderstandings or alienate team members.

4. **Role of Mindfulness:** Recognizing and addressing the need for patience and presence in group settings helps foster trust, deeper engagement, and more effective communication.

5. **Mentorship as a Mirror:** Learning from a mentor's ability to be fully engaged and calm can inspire self-reflection and encourage meaningful behavioral change.

6. **Balancing Speed with Collaboration:** While speed has its place, creating space for others to process and contribute at their own pace can unlock creativity, innovation, and stronger team outcomes.

7. **Work in Progress:** Personal growth often requires sustained effort. Acknowledging oneself as a "work in progress" allows room for development while maintaining the strength of natural abilities.

8. **Strategic Slowdown:** Deliberately slowing down at key moments enhances understanding, strengthens relationships, and ultimately improves the quality and impact of collective work.

9. **New Definition of Speed:** True speed isn't just about how quickly tasks are completed but also about the efficiency and quality of collaboration and outcomes.

Time Management:

Micromanager vs. Strategic Leader:

Six months into my mentoring journey, I found myself deeply introspecting and identifying behaviors that were holding me back. Speed, a long-standing strength, had already been flagged and addressed to some extent. I was learning to give my team more time, to listen better. Yet, my calendar told a different story. It was still perpetually packed—a relentless sea of meetings and reviews.

When I raised this with my mentor, she smiled knowingly. "Time management is one of the greatest challenges leaders face," she said. "Mastering it often separates good leaders from great ones." Her questions made me pause and think about what was causing my calendar to spiral out of control.

As we dissected the issue, a clear pattern emerged. My need for frequent reviews, born from a zest for perfection and a fear of suboptimal outcomes, was consuming an inordinate amount of time. I was micromanaging, even if unintentionally. My days were filled with reviewing tasks my team was fully capable of handling. The truth was sobering, I was stuck in the weeds, leaving little room for the larger responsibilities of leadership.

The first step was to reclaim my time. I began by blocking "think time" on my calendar—periods where no meetings were allowed. But this wasn't as straightforward as it seemed. Despite the blocks, people continued to walk in, seeking reviews or discussions. And I, all too eager to solve problems, entertained these interruptions, rendering my so-called 'think time' meaningless.

It became clear that my time management woes stemmed not just from external demands but from internal fears. My fear of letting go. My reluctance to let go, and be reassured that work was on track. I realized that before I could manage my calendar, I needed to address my approach and mindset.

I was leading a team of leaders, many of whom managed large teams themselves. These were capable individuals, perfectly able to own their work and deliver results. My role wasn't to do their jobs for them; it was to guide, support, and create an environment where they could thrive.

My mentor's advice was simple yet profound: "There are some things you'll want to see done with perfection. The rest, you must let go."

With that in mind, I took deliberate steps to delegate more effectively. I communicated clear expectations to my team and set boundaries around my availability. I blocked off specific times for pre-aligned discussions and reviews, making it clear that they should manage day-to-day tasks independently. Regular one-on-one meetings and informal coffee chats ensured I remained accessible for guidance and connection, but the constant stream of interruptions was curtailed.

At first, it was challenging. My instinct to step in and "fix" things was hard to suppress. But over time, I found a balance that worked for me. I focused on the key priorities where my input was truly necessary and let them take ownership of the rest.

The results were almost immediate. Within a month, I began to feel a sense of relief. The constant burnout faded, replaced by a newfound clarity. My team, empowered to lead their projects, began delivering results with the same finesse I'd once insisted on. The difference? They were doing it independently, and often, exceeding my expectations.

With fewer interruptions and a lighter calendar, I had the mental bandwidth to engage in meaningful conversations with my team. I could spend time reflecting, exploring strategic opportunities, and expanding my circle of influence. Not only was the work getting done, but we were thriving as a team.

Key Takeaways:

1. **Time Management Starts with a Mindset:** Addressing internal fears and trusting your team are critical to reclaiming control of your time.

2. **Delegate Effectively:** Focus on key priorities that require your attention and empower your team to handle the rest.

3. **Establish Boundaries:** Block think time and communicate clear expectations to avoid unnecessary interruptions.

4. **Quality Over Quantity:** Fewer, well-structured interactions can lead to deeper connections and better results.

5. **Create Space for Strategic Thinking:** Freeing up your calendar allows you to focus on high-impact activities and long-term goals.

By focusing on priorities and letting go of unnecessary involvement, I not only improved my time management but also became a better leader. The journey from micromanager to strategic leader wasn't easy, but it was worth every step.

Juggling Multiple Balls:

Balancing personal and professional priorities is one of the most complex challenges we face today. The demands of work, family, and personal aspirations often clash, leaving us feeling strained and stretched. This constant push-and-pull can quietly seep into our behavior, making us less patient, more anxious, and less present. It's important to recognize that excelling as a leader at work becomes nearly impossible if our personal life is weighed down by unresolved challenges.

For years, I had been a devoted mother. My evenings and weekends were dedicated to my twin boys, Arun and Varun. I loved spending time with them—watching them grow, ensuring we dined together, watching movies, traveling, reviewing school assignments, and nurturing their dreams. But as they entered their teenage years, the dynamics shifted. Their schooling became more intense, and as a single parent, I found myself struggling to ensure they spent enough time practicing and completing their schoolwork.

It wasn't that I stopped being present, but I felt like I wasn't doing enough. Despite my best efforts, their academic discipline seemed to falter, and I couldn't help but feel dissatisfied with myself as a parent. This gnawing sense of inadequacy followed me to work.

This sense of imbalance grew more pronounced over time. I watched as my male colleagues freely voiced their personal challenges—taking time off for a parent-teacher meeting or a family appointment without hesitation. Yet, for me, the story felt different. Like many women, I hesitated to admit how loudly my personal life was calling for attention.

I feared it would make me seem less capable or committed at work. Instead, I managed these struggles silently, juggling responsibilities without asking for help or advice.

The truth is, personal challenges come in many forms. It might be a parent struggling with a child's academic discipline, a caregiver worried about an aging parent's health, or someone navigating the complexities of a relationship. No matter what the situation, it's impossible to entirely block these challenges from creeping into our work life. Whether we acknowledge it or not, they affect our thoughts, energy, and overall demeanor.

I realized this more clearly than ever when I decided to confide in my mentor. It took weeks to summon the courage—I worried about being judged, about appearing less capable. But the weight of carrying it all alone had become too much. When I finally opened up, it felt like a release.

My mentor, a mother herself, listened patiently and without judgment. She didn't offer a ready-made solution but shared her own struggles and helped me reframe my perspective. She pointed out something that resonated deeply: while some children are naturally self-driven, others need more guidance until they find their rhythm. For my boys, supervision and structure were essential at this stage. Even though they were now into their teens, they simply needed reinforcement of regular post-school self-study time and clear boundaries to limit digital distractions.

Through this simple mother-to-mother chat, I gained clarity. It was a rare moment in my otherwise largely corporate life, where such sharing and reflections rarely occur. What stood out to me was how important it is to have someone to talk to—someone who can provide perspective and advice when personal challenges begin to spill into work. Left unaddressed, these worries linger in the back of your mind, quietly impacting your focus and presence.

Since then, I've made a conscious effort to prioritize being home on time. Even if it means carrying work home or taking conference calls from home. My presence ensures Arun and Varun study. I sit next to them doing my work, with an oversight and periodic check-ins on their tasks. Just being present, keeping their distractions at bay, and ensuring they complete their regular classwork has brought a sense of order to the chaos—and it has made me feel much better too.

What I've taken away from this journey is the importance of balance, not as a static state but as a dynamic process. Life's demands will never perfectly align, but acknowledging and addressing our personal priorities can make us better leaders, parents, and individuals. When we stop trying to compartmentalize and instead embrace the interconnectedness of our roles, we can begin to truly thrive.

Key Takeaways from the Chapter "Juggling Multiple Balls":

1. **Personal and Professional Lives Are Interconnected:** It's nearly impossible to separate personal challenges from work. Unresolved personal issues can subtly impact focus, patience, and overall effectiveness at work.

2. **Acknowledging Personal Challenges Is Not a Weakness:** Sharing personal struggles or seeking advice doesn't make you less capable or committed. Instead, it's a necessary step toward finding clarity and balance.

3. **Having Someone to Talk to Is Crucial:** Confiding in a trusted mentor, colleague, or friend can provide valuable perspective and guidance. It's important to have a sounding board when personal challenges begin to affect your professional life.

4. **Balancing Work and Family Is a Dynamic Process:** Balance isn't about perfection but about making deliberate choices to address priorities. It's a continuous effort that requires flexibility and mindfulness.

5. **Presence Matters:** For both work and family, being present—physically and mentally—has a significant impact. Small adjustments, like dedicating focused time to children or team members, can create meaningful results.

6. **Focus on Common Purpose, Not Judgments:** When dealing with challenges at home or work, staying objective and focusing on shared goals helps in addressing issues constructively without letting emotions cloud judgment.

7. **Parenting Requires Adaptability:** Children's needs evolve as they grow, and parenting strategies must

adapt to provide the right balance of guidance, structure, and independence.

8. **Seeking Order Amid Chaos Helps:** Establishing routines and addressing priorities head-on can reduce mental clutter and create a sense of calm. This clarity enhances both personal and professional performance.

9. **Self-Compassion is Essential:** Feeling inadequate or stretched thin is natural in the face of competing priorities. Recognizing that no one can do everything perfectly is key to maintaining mental and emotional well-being.

10. **Leadership Improves Through Balance:** Addressing personal priorities doesn't detract from professional effectiveness; instead, it enhances focus, decision-making, and leadership by creating a more grounded and centered mindset.

Being the Charismatic Leader:

Climbing the ladder of leadership is a journey many of us aspire to undertake. Beyond appearances, speech, and gestures, the essence of charisma lies in how a leader makes others feel. Charismatic leaders leave you energized, inspired, and often propel you to think in directions you hadn't considered before.

During one of my leadership assessments, my counselor posed a pivotal question: "Richa, you need to think about what you want to do next. Where do you want to go from here?" It wasn't just a question; it was a challenge. Around this time, I was fortunate to have a mentor who became a true sounding board for me. She didn't hand me solutions on a platter. Instead, she made me think deeply, sparking motivation within me to strive for more.

Her charisma wasn't loud or flamboyant. It was grounded, engaging, and inspiring. Each conversation left me feeling energized and ready to improve myself. I realized then that charisma isn't just about natural magnetism; it's a skill you can cultivate—a combination of presence, empathy, and the ability to inspire.

One trait that also stands out in charismatic leaders is that they stay calm. Whether in high-pressure meetings or casual discussions, their calm demeanor is striking. Their facial expressions rarely give away any emotions, making them seem grounded and approachable. Of course, extreme situations sometimes called for visible emotions, but these moments were exceptions.

This calmness was something I had to work on. While I managed to stay composed in larger meetings, smaller settings revealed my tendency to take charge and let emotions slip through. True calmness, I realized, couldn't be faked. It required inner peace, clarity of thought, and genuine engagement with the present moment.

Many advocate for mindfulness or meditation, but those practices didn't resonate with me. As someone with high energy and a constant urge to do, I needed a different approach. What worked for me was dialing back my constant engagement with work. I started taking planned breaks—unplugging from emails and calls—and prioritized physical fitness, which had taken a back seat in recent years.

I also focused on settling things at home, spending quality time with my kids, and organizing my surroundings. With a better-planned calendar that allocated time for all aspects of my life—fitness, family, and even mundane tasks like tidying up—I began to declutter my mind. This, in turn, brought a sense of contentment and presence.

I became calmer in meetings, genuinely happier, and eager to share that positivity with others. I no longer rushed through discussions; instead, I relished the process of listening and engaging. While I still offered ideas and solutions, my calm demeanor allowed me to be more engaged, listen and build better connections.

Looking back, I wish I had embraced this shift earlier. Patience, calmness, and living in the moment have not only made me a better leader but also freed up time to accomplish more.

Charisma, I've learned, isn't an inherent trait reserved for a select few. It's cultivated through presence, self-reflection, and a genuine desire to uplift others. By embodying these qualities, you can become a leader who inspires, energizes, and leaves a lasting impact.

Key Takeaways:

1. **Charisma is about how you make others feel:** Energizing and inspiring others is a hallmark of a charismatic leader.

2. **Calmness is a cornerstone of charisma:** It requires inner peace, clarity, and a present mindset—not just a façade of composure.

3. **Reflection fuels transformation:** Scaling back from constant activity allows for strategic thinking and meaningful influence.

4. **Personal balance enhances professional impact:** Prioritizing fitness, family, and mental clarity can transform your leadership presence.

5. **Charisma is a skill you can develop:** Through self-awareness, genuine engagement, and the ability to inspire, anyone can grow into a charismatic leader.

Hidden Agendas, Half-Truths, and Stories:

I take pride in being a direct and straightforward person—someone who speaks her mind and addresses concerns openly. Clear communication and standing up for the truth have always been my guiding principles. However, this approach had its challenges. I often found myself emotionally drained after dealing with individuals who were indirect, indulged in gossip, or operated with hidden agendas. Their behavior unsettled me, disrupting my peace of mind and leaving me feeling weighed down.

One turning point came during a workshop I attended. As we discussed workplace challenges, I shared my frustration with the facilitator. "It's exhausting," I admitted, "dealing with dishonesty or hidden agendas. I can't help but feel unsettled when people avoid addressing issues head-on."

The facilitator listened thoughtfully and then offered a response that caught me off guard: "Richa, not everyone is strong enough to confront issues or speak their truth. People behave differently, often shaped by their experiences. Instead of judging their intentions, try to appreciate their differences and focus on what they bring to the table."

Her advice made sense, but it left me feeling unsettled. Was I supposed to ignore behaviors that disrupted my energy and the team's harmony? The conversation felt incomplete, as though it hadn't fully addressed my concerns.

A few years later, I found myself wrestling with the same issue. This time, I brought it up with my mentor, hoping for deeper insights. My mentor echoed the facilitator's sentiment but added a practical dimension. "Each person is different," he said, "and as a leader, you need to stay objective about the team's goals and performance. While behaviors like gossip or avoidance can be draining, focusing on them won't help you. Instead, center your energy on measurable results and set clear expectations for acceptable ways of working."

They also suggested a pragmatic approach: assess the extent to which certain behaviors harm the team. If an individual's actions significantly disrupt team dynamics, address the issue directly. However, not every quirk requires confrontation; sometimes, it's about managing around the behavior while keeping the team's objectives in focus.

This perspective gradually shifted my approach. I began to see people not as problems to solve but as individuals with unique strengths, weaknesses, and experiences. We may not always like how someone operates, but by staying focused on shared goals and maintaining emotional detachment, we can work together more effectively.

One example stands out vividly. I once worked with a colleague who avoided direct confrontation and preferred communicating through intermediaries. Initially, his approach frustrated me—it felt inefficient and evasive. But instead of letting my frustration fester, I decided to have an honest conversation with him. What I learned surprised me: his avoidance stemmed from past experiences where his directness had been dismissed or ridiculed. By creating a safe space for open dialogue and setting boundaries around communication, we were able to collaborate more effectively.

Another instance involved a team member who frequently engaged in office gossip. It made me unhappy, wanting to distance myself from this colleague, but I decided to take a different approach. I redirected our conversations toward constructive feedback about their work and highlighted their contributions. Over time, I noticed a shift—they began focusing more on their tasks and less on negative talk.

Through these experiences, I realized the secret to navigating challenges lies in focusing on *why* we're working together: achieving shared goals. It's not about ignoring disruptive behaviors or tolerating toxic patterns, but about giving people a fair chance to align with the team's purpose.

By keeping emotions in check, communicating openly, and creating a supportive environment, we can foster a culture of growth and collaboration. Sometimes, it's about setting boundaries; other times, it's about understanding the "why" behind someone's behavior. And when necessary, it's about addressing the issue firmly yet fairly.

Ultimately, the lesson is this: leadership isn't about changing people; it's about navigating differences, fostering mutual respect, and ensuring the team moves forward together.

Key Takeaways:

1. **Stay Objective:** Focus on shared goals and measurable results rather than personal frustrations or gossip.

2. **Provide a Nurturing Environment:** Ensure every individual has a fair chance to thrive before making judgments.

3. **Communicate Openly:** Honest conversations can reveal underlying reasons for behaviors and help establish better working relationships.

4. **Appreciate Differences:** Not everyone operates the same way; valuing diversity in approaches can strengthen the team.

5. **Address Issues Strategically:** Assess the impact of negative behaviors on the team before taking decisive action.

6. **Maintain Emotional Detachment:** Avoid letting emotions cloud judgment when dealing with challenging individuals.

7. **Redirect Negative Energy:** Use constructive feedback to shift focus from unproductive behaviors to meaningful contributions.

Breaking Barriers:

This is a sensitive topic, one I've wrestled with for years. I've always believed in leaning in—playing by the rules of the game to succeed. "Be a wolf in a pack of wolves," I'd tell myself, adapting to the environment to win. Yet, as I've climbed the professional ladder, I've come to see that no matter how adaptable you are, there's no denying the differences in how men and women think, work, and are perceived.

Our brains are wired differently. We process situations differently. And these differences inevitably influence our decisions, behaviors, and how others respond to us. When I've brought up this topic with men, the initial reaction is often denial. "Bias doesn't exist anymore," they say. Some, usually those with working spouses or daughters stepping into the workforce, may concede, "Yes, there's some bias, but things are changing." Yet, their acknowledgment rarely goes beyond words; systemic change remains elusive.

I remember one conversation in particular with a senior colleague. He dismissed my concerns with a laugh and said, "Isn't it great that women are getting so many opportunities now?" The comment, well-meaning on the surface, stung. It ignored the underlying challenges—the battles fought daily to be heard, respected, and seen as equals.

A stark example of this double standard is how assertiveness, drive, and passion are perceived in men versus women. When a man sets boundaries or pushes for excellence, he's seen as a strong leader, driven and focused. However, when a woman exhibits the same traits, she's often labeled aggressive or short-tempered. I remember a meeting where I firmly disagreed with a strategy proposal, laying out logical reasons and offering alternatives. While my male counterpart was commended for his "vision," I was later described as being "too forceful." It was disheartening but also enlightening—it showed me how ingrained these biases are.

To handle such situations, I've learned to approach them with both clarity and composure. Remaining calm while reinforcing your points with data and logic often neutralizes emotional misinterpretation. Additionally, involving allies in discussions—whether mentors, colleagues, or team members—can amplify your voice and add credibility. Finally, addressing feedback directly can help recalibrate perceptions. For instance, after that meeting, I asked a trusted colleague for feedback and used it to refine my delivery while staying true to my assertiveness. Over time, I've learned that consistency in how you communicate and deliver results gradually shifts perceptions.

Through discussions with mentors and counselors, I've gained a clearer perspective on these issues. One mentor gave me advice that has stayed with me: "Bias is everywhere, but awareness is the first step to mitigating its impact. It's not about denying its existence but about understanding how to navigate it." This shifted my approach from frustration to strategy.

Bias, after all, isn't always overt. It's woven into the fabric of our social conditioning. Even as children, we're subtly taught roles that reinforce stereotypes. The nurse is a woman; the pilot is a man. These narratives seep into adulthood, shaping how we perceive ourselves and others.

I've come to realize that bias isn't limited to men. Women, too, carry subconscious biases, often against their own gender. I've seen women struggle to take orders from a female leader or accept constructive feedback. This internalized bias complicates the already challenging dynamics women face in leadership roles.

For a time, these biases bogged me down. I questioned myself, wondered if I was doing enough, or if I was imagining the subtle slights and resistance. But over time, and with guidance from mentors, I learned to approach bias differently.

One of the most valuable lessons I've learned is the power of gentle confrontation. For example, when team members failed to follow through on instructions, I stopped assuming malice or disrespect. Instead, I began asking open-ended questions like, "Can you walk me through why this wasn't completed?" or "What support do you need to align better next time?" This not only diffused tension but also set a tone of accountability and collaboration.

With new teams, I've found that clear expectations and recap discussions are critical. Building systems that promote accountability minimizes misunderstandings and ensures alignment, creating a more productive and respectful environment.

Bias is deeply ingrained, and the journey to address it can be exhausting. But I've realized that denial or avoidance only amplifies its impact. By acknowledging bias and working around it—rather than against it—I've found ways to be effective without letting it define my journey.

One moment stands out: a colleague once said to me, "You make it look easy." I smiled, knowing the truth. It isn't easy, but that's not the point. The point is to keep going, to stay focused, and to leave the door open a little wider for the women who come after us. The goal isn't just to win within the system but to inspire gradual change—step by step, conversation by conversation.

Navigating bias requires self-awareness, adaptability, and strategic action. It's about finding the balance between playing the game and rewriting the rules, creating space for progress while achieving your goals. And perhaps most importantly, it's about staying true to yourself in the process.

Key Takeaways:

1. **Adapt Your Communication for Effectiveness:** Clear, calm, and data-driven communication can help neutralize misinterpretations of assertiveness. Gentle confrontation and open-ended questions can create a more collaborative and respectful environment.

2. **Consistency Shifts Perception:** Consistently delivering results and maintaining a balanced approach to communication can gradually reshape how assertive women are perceived in the workplace.

3. **Channel Energy into Systems, Not Conflicts:** Instead of getting drawn into unnecessary conflicts, focus on creating systems that promote accountability and clarity. Let your work and results speak for themselves.

4. **Bias Affects Everyone, Including Women:** Subconscious biases aren't limited to men; women can also carry biases, making leadership roles even more challenging. Awareness and openness to feedback are vital to addressing these biases.

5. **Mentorship and Support Are Critical:** Conversations with mentors and trusted colleagues can provide valuable strategies and frameworks for navigating biases and challenges in the workplace.

6. **Set Clear Expectations and Boundaries:** Establishing clear communication guidelines and expectations with team members minimizes misunderstandings and fosters accountability.

7. **Focus on Shared Goals:** By keeping emotions in check and prioritizing shared objectives, you can foster collaboration and minimize the impact of biases on team dynamics.

8. **Inspire Gradual Change:** The goal isn't just to succeed within the current system but to pave the way for gradual change, creating a more inclusive and supportive environment for future generations.

Section 3

Mentoring is for Life

Self-Awareness Through Mentoring: Navigating Change and Growth:

Life is an ever-changing journey, where no single solution fits every situation. We often find ourselves facing unfamiliar circumstances that require us to adapt, evolve, and sometimes reimagine our approach. It helps therefore to actively seek out mentors as we move through different life and stages of career.

When I transitioned from being a manager to taking on a leadership role, the way I approached challenges needed a complete shift. What worked as a manager—focused on processes, results, and day-to-day problem-solving—no longer sufficed when leading teams at a strategic level. The change required self-awareness, and then strength to let go, of what worked in the past. Gathering that strength for me, became easier when echoed by my mentor.

As a manager, I believed in hands-on involvement. I would oversee the details of projects, ensuring my team stayed on track. This approach worked well in delivering results but didn't leave much room for team autonomy. When I stepped into a larger leadership role, however, I quickly realized that micromanaging wasn't sustainable. The scope of responsibilities had expanded, and I required me to delegate effectively, and at the same time enable and energize to ensure I got the needed results.

I managed, but initially with a lot of heart burn. There were times, where I would feel burnt out, and at times worry about the quality of results. At times I also struggled to let go.

I was fortunate to have a mentor I could confide in. She encouraged me to focus on empowering my team by setting clear expectations and stepping back to allow them to lead. "Your role as a leader is to inspire and enable, not control," she said. This advice prompted me to reflect on my tendency to intervene too often and shift my approach to one of support and guidance. The result? My team began to thrive, bringing innovative solutions to the table, while I could focus on strategic decision-making.

The Power of a Sounding Board:

Mentoring reminds us that growth is not about having all the answers but about asking the right questions and being willing to adapt. By reflecting on my journey from manager to leader, I've realized that self-awareness is a continuous process. It's about recognizing when an old approach no longer serves you and having the courage to evolve.

Being on a mentoring journey keeps us awake to ourselves, our purpose and things we must do to reach our goals.

It has helped me stay more mindful about my bias for speed, especially when it comes to interactions with people and team, I remind myself that I need to give this time.

As leaders, we frequently need to deal with team members, who may have performance or behavior issues, or at times both. In absence of lessons learnt through mentoring I would have simply scheduled a meeting with a team member, not performing up to the mark, and had a very specific performance and goal centric discussion. I am now more aware and mindful, of the fact, that each person is different and its first important to understand what's driving or working against that person.

Now, I usually have such dialogues, over a cup of coffee, where my team member is at ease, and can open up and share issues, or ask for help and we can mutually work on best possible outcomes.

As life changes, so do our roles, challenges, and opportunities. Self-awareness helps us stay grounded, while mentoring provides the tools to navigate these transitions with confidence and grace. Together, they create a powerful framework for personal and professional growth, enabling us to face change not as a hurdle but as a chance to become better versions of ourselves.

Mentors as Networking Catalysts:

One of the most powerful, yet often overlooked, aspects of mentoring is its role in expanding professional networks. A mentor does more than just offer advice—they open doors, make introductions, and provide access to opportunities that might otherwise remain out of reach. Effective mentoring doesn't just prepare mentees for the next step; it also positions them in the right rooms with the right people to take that step confidently.

Every mentor comes with a wealth of connections—colleagues, industry peers, former managers, and even mentees from years past. Leveraging these networks, mentors can:

- Connect mentees to influencers or decision-makers in their field.

- Facilitate introductions that align with the mentee's career goals.

- Provide warm recommendations that carry weight in professional circles.

The value of such introductions cannot be overstated. An industry veteran's endorsement can often accomplish in minutes what might take years for a mentee to achieve on their own.

I can share an example of when I was mentoring a young professional. He was a talented analyst looking to break into the tech industry, but his network was limited to the finance world. I knew the CTO of a mid-sized tech company.

I invited my mentee to accompany me to a conference where this CTO was speaking. Finding a private moment, I introduced my mentee to the CTO, talking about his knack for using data to solve complex problems. That introduction led to a follow-up conversation, and eventually a job, my mentee really wanted. As a mentor, i facilitated the process, my mentee owned and drove it.

Networking through mentorship often has a cascading impact. A single introduction can lead to a web of connections, opening unforeseen opportunities. It's not just about who the mentor knows but about how those connections expand the mentee's reach over time.

As you reflect on your mentoring journey, remember this: A network isn't just a list of contacts—it's a living, breathing ecosystem. And as a mentor, you have the privilege and power to help someone thrive within it, and as a mentee, you can safely ask for help and guidance on how to expand your ecosystem.

Ending Note:

As I reflect on my journey, one truth stands out: the energy you allow into your life shapes your path. I have learned to keep negative energy at bay, letting go of judgment and resentment. Each person is different, shaped by their own experiences, beliefs, and agendas. Disagreements are inevitable, and others' motivations may not always align with your own. But to achieve your purpose and find success, it is crucial to rise above these emotions.

I have stopped judging people for their actions and instead focus on the bigger picture—on what I need to achieve and what works best for the business. Acceptance has become a cornerstone of my approach. By understanding and embracing differences, I have found greater clarity and peace.

Letting go of negative emotions is not about complacency but about empowerment. Staying positive creates a ripple effect. It brings more energy, makes challenges feel surmountable, and frees the mind to innovate and excel. Positivity is not just a strategy; it is the foundation of a better and greater version of yourself.

To anyone reading this, I encourage you to cultivate positivity in your journey. Shed the weight of negativity, embrace the differences around you, and focus on your purpose. In doing so, you'll unlock a resilience and energy that propel you toward not just success but fulfilment. Positivity is the start of a brighter, stronger, and more impactful you.

About the Author

Richa is an inspiring leader, and a business coach with wealth of experience across multinationals and startups, leading both small and large businesses with teams exceeding 1,000 people.

She is a management graduate from the prestigious IIM Bangalore and alumnus of Wharton Business School.

Her story is one of resilience and determination. As she climbed the corporate ladder, Richa simultaneously juggled a series of personal challenges, including balancing the needs of her ageing parents, sister and the endless energy of her young twin boys. Through it all, she faced moments of doubt, vulnerability, and hardship.

In this book, Richa opens her heart and shares her most vulnerable moments, showing how finding the right mentors not only help her afloat, but helped her fly. She speaks candidly about the power of mentorship in shaping her journey, offering readers a roadmap to discover their own paths, no matter how daunting the challenges they face.

Her words aim to inspire readers to embrace their struggles, seek guidance, and find the courage to keep moving forward. This book is not just a guide to professional success—it's a heartfelt invitation to rise above life's challenges and create a life of purpose and fulfilment.

84